Birds

What are birds? 2

Storks 3

Woodpeckers 4

Puffins 5

Ostriches 6

Owls 8

Parrots 9

Where are birds? 10

Story: The Mysterious Egg 11

Activities 25

Picture Dictionary 30

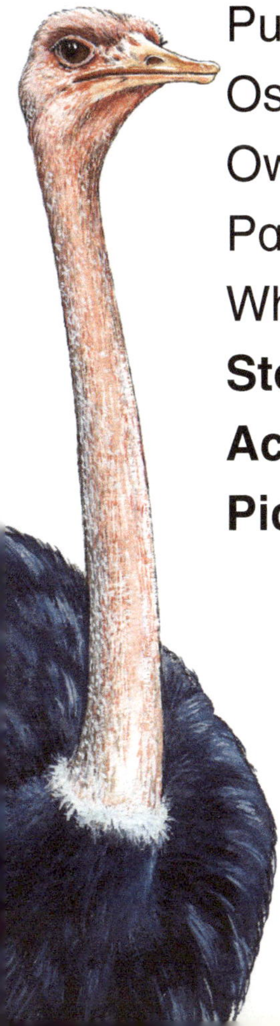

Written by Mark Ormerod

Illustrated by Red Giraffe

What are birds?

Birds are animals. They've got beaks, wings and feathers.

Storks

This bird is a stork. It's got black and white feathers, a red beak and orange legs. It lives in a big nest with all its family. It eats fish.

You can see stork nests on houses in Spain.

Woodpeckers

This bird is a woodpecker.
It's got black, white and red feathers.
It lives in trees and it eats insects.

You can't see the woodpecker's nest. It's inside the tree.

Puffins

This is a puffin. It's a funny bird. It's got black and white feathers, orange feet and a red and black beak. It lives on rocks by the sea. It eats fish.

Ostriches

Ostriches are very big birds. They live in Africa. They eat grass and insects.

A mother ostrich has got brown feathers. A father ostrich has got black and white feathers.

Ostriches can't fly, but they can run very fast. They can run at 65 kilometres an hour!

Owls

This bird is an owl. It's got brown and white feathers. It lives in trees. It eats meat.

Owls sleep in the day. They fly at night.

Parrots

This bird is a parrot. It's got red, blue and yellow feathers. It lives in trees. It eats fruit.

Where are birds?

At the zoo you can see birds from around the world. But birds are everywhere – in the park, on the beach ... just look!

The Mysterious Egg

Written by Mark Ormerod
Illustrated by Red Giraffe

It's Saturday. Vicky and Bobby are in the park.

Vicky and Bobby can't find the football.

Vicky picks the egg up.

The children look at the trees.

At home, Dad puts the egg in a box.

They put the box under a radiator.

The children look at the book.

They look on the computer.

Then Bobby sees a photograph in the newspaper.

Vicky, Bobby and their dad go to the zoo with the egg. The zoo keeper is very happy.

He puts the egg in the flamingo's nest.

The mother flamingo is very happy.

She sits on the egg to keep it warm.

One week later, Vicky and Bobby have got a present and a card. Vicky opens the card.

Bobby opens the present.

Activities

1 Match the birds to the sentences.

1 

2 

3 

4 

5 

6 

This is a stork. [ ]	This is a woodpecker. [ ]	This is a parrot. [ ]
This is an owl. [ ]	This is an ostrich. [ ]	This is a puffin. [1]

2 Complete the sentences.

grass

meat

~~insects~~

fruit

fish

1 A woodpecker eats insects .

2 A puffin eats ____________________ .

3 An ostrich eats ____________________ .

4 A parrot eats ____________________ .

5 An owl eats ____________________ .

3 Write the words.

4 Circle T (True) or F (False).

1	An ostrich can't fly.	(T)	F
2	An owl sleeps at night.	T	F
3	A parrot can learn to say words.	T	F
4	A puffin can swim underwater.	T	F
5	A woodpecker lives on rocks.	T	F
6	A father ostrich has got brown feathers.	T	F

5 Complete the sentences with the words in the box.

eggs	box	happy	zoo	~~park~~	newspaper

1 Vicky and Bobby find an egg in the park.

2 Dad puts the egg in a ____________.

3 The children find out about birds ____________.

4 Bobby sees a photograph in the ____________.

5 The children and their dad go to the ____________.

6 The mother flamingo is very ____________.

6 Complete the sentences with the words in the box.

in	under	on

1 The football is in the tree.

2 The football is ____________ the bird.

3 The football is ____________ the computer.

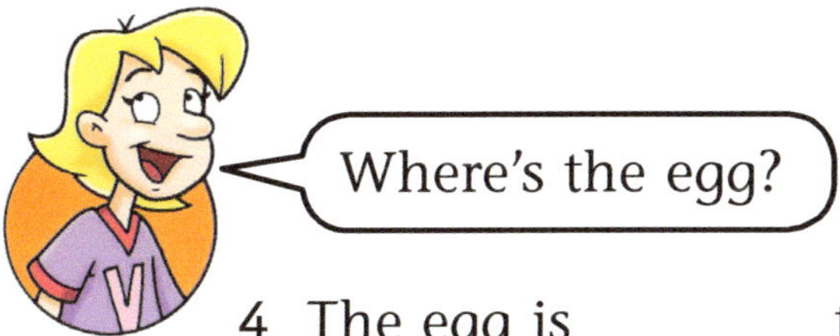

4 The egg is ________ the radiator.

5 The egg is ________ the box.

6 The egg is ________ the nest.

7 Who says it? Match the speech bubbles to Bobby, Vicky or Dad.

An ostrich's egg is very big.

I can play football very well.

Let's find out about birds eggs.

It's important to keep the egg warm.

It isn't under the trees.

Is it a woodpecker's egg?

8 Write and find the secret word.

1

2

3

1

2 h a p p y

3

4

5

6

4

5

6

What's the secret word? ____________________

9 Complete with the words in the box.

feet	feathers	~~flamingo~~	beak	legs

This bird is a ___flamingo___.

It's got a black and grey ________.

It's got pink and black ________.

It's got orange ________ and

________.

10 Complete the sentences.

This bird is a ________

It's got ________

____

It lives ________

____

It eats ________

____

Picture Dictionary

beak

wing

feather

nest

fish

tree

insects

rocks

swim

grass

fly

run

meat

fruit

park

beach

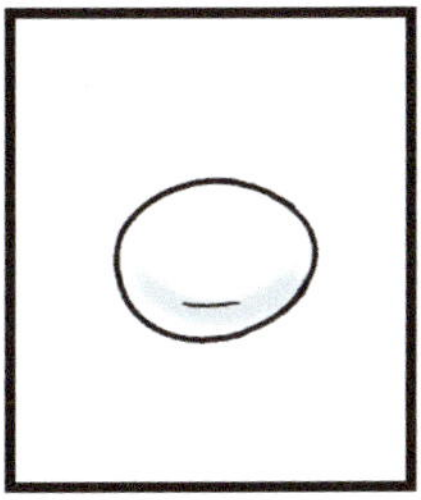
egg

football

pick up

box

radiator

book

computer

photograph

newspaper

flamingo

zoo keeper

happy

present

card

Easter egg

chocolate

Macmillan Education
4 Crinan Street,
London N1 9XW
A division of Macmillan Publishers Limited
Companies and representatives throughout the world

ISBN 978 0 2300 1012 3

First published 2007

Illustrated by Red Giraffe Limited

The author and publishers would like to thank the following for permission to reproduce their photographic material:

Cover Photography Getty Images/yanta

FLPA/ Duncan usher/ Foto Natura p2, FLPA/ Yva Momatiuk/ John Eastcott/ Minden Pictures p5, FLPA/ Cyril Ruoso/ JH Editorial/ Minden Pictures p10tl, FLPA/ Alamy Stock Photo/Jean Landry p10tr; Alamy Stock Photo/MIHAI ANDRITOIU p9b; NHPA/ Martin Harvey p3b&t, Getty Images/James Warwick p6 & 7, NHPA/ Paul Brough p6b, NHPA/ Stephen Dalton p8, Getty Images/Heather Paul p10b; Alamy Stock Photo/Abi Warner Photography p4, Getty Images/MARS/ paulafrench p7t, Getty Images/M AMIR FAQIH/500px

Printed and bound in Brazil

2024
8